I Am California™

For information contact:

I Am America Books, LLC
P.O Box 26480
Scottsdale, AZ 85255
www.IAmAmericaBooks.com

ISBN 978-0-9844754-1-4

Printed in China

I Am™ California
Part of the I Am America™ Series By Hugh K. Tirrell

"Share the wonders of our United States with your family"

Our country is amazing and unique.

Few people know much about the state they live in or other states.

The "I Am America"™ books teach families about the variety and similarities that make up our country.

We are an amalgamation of fifty states, each inhabited by ancestors from many countries.

Every state has a different past, present and future. Each looks different from the other.

Inhabitants often speak differently.

A Mainer doesn't sound like a Texan. The Illinois landscape doesn't look like Oregon.

The primary animals and fish of Maryland differ from those of California.

The "I Am America"™ books focus on the geology and geography of each state.

Modern human beings and modern man-made structures are not featured unless they are an iconic

part of the state, such as California's Golden Gate Bridge.

The books also include information about the states animals, birds, fish and trees as well as it's first

human inhabitants - the American Indians. Historical events are occasionally covered.

The "I Am America"™ books will remain current and be treasured by your family for generations.

Instructions to the Reader

This book is written as a script and intended to be read aloud.

The state and other "inhabitants" are cast as characters in a play to be enacted by the reader(s).

The plants, animals and trees talk to the child, sharing interesting facts about themselves and friends.

So PERFORM the characters as you read! Give each character a different voice.

This icon will cue you as to which character is speaking. *CALIFORNIA Says...*

Your children may wish to contribute their own voices as they learn the book.

Above all, HAVE FUN WITH THE VOICES!

GIANT SEQUOIA Says...

Hi *(Name of child)...*
I'm called Sequoia.

Personalize the experience by inserting the name of your child when you see *(name)*.

Use the gender of your child when you encounter *(his/her...brother/sister...he/she)*.

Each book is loaded with learning opportunities for children and adults alike.

The images will stimulate discussion on colors, shapes and names of objects.

Older children and adults can discuss the land and its non-human inhabitants and how we humans can protect our environment.

A younger child may not have the attention span to read the entire book in one sitting.

The book is broken into segments. Read one segment. If your child is still enjoying the book, read another segment. If not, pick it up later. Above all, enjoy this bonding experience!

It's a magic gift – time with your child.

CALIFORNIA Says...

Hi! My name is CALIFORNIA!

What is your name?

Nice to meet you *(name of child)*.

Will you be my friend? I hope so.

4

CALIFORNIA Says...

I'm excited to show you my many beautiful places and for you to meet many of my friends.

My Animal Friends

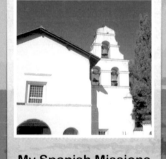

My Spanish Missions

My Majestic Mountains

My Tree Friends

My Ocean Friends

My Bird Friends

5

I am California!

I am a state in The United States of America.

How many brothers and sisters do you have *(name of child)*?

California

Eureka

San Francisco
Oakland

Santa Cruz

Monterey

The Original Seal of California

31st State
Admitted 1850

Angeles

San Diego

Today I have 49 other brothers and sisters.

Together we make up our great country.

We're all very different but I'm just going to tell you about me...

I AM CALIFORNIA!

Only two brothers/sisters - Alaska and Texas - are bigger than me.

Are you the biggest in your family, *(name of child)*?

No! Who is?

I have given our country two U.S. Presidents:

Richard M. Nixon
37th presiden
1969-1974

Ronald R. Reagan
40th President
1981-89

Ronald Reagan was also my
Governor for eight years.

6

Before I became a state, I was part of Mexico.

Many of my people wanted to be free from Mexico.

They created a flag with a bear on it to inspire them to win freedom.

See the red star? That is the same lone star another brother/sister named Texas used on their flag when they won freedom from Mexico.

The bear is one of my big animal friends.

The flag says "California Republic." That's what I was before becoming a state in 1850.

CALIFORNIA

This is what the U.S. flag looked like when I became a state.

How many stars do you see?

That's right. There were only 31 stars. They represented the 31 states we had when I joined the United States.

7

California Black Bear

CALIFORNIA Says...

I am CALIFORNIA, and as I said, I am BIG...
I have the BIGGEST animals on land.

8

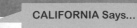

CALIFORNIA Says...

And I have the biggest ocean animals living in my Pacific Ocean.

Naturally, the Pacific is the BIGGEST ocean in the whole wide world!

Humpback Whale

9

CALIFORNIA Says...

I have the BIGGEST trees...

My redwoods are the tallest. Many are over 300 feet tall.

10

And my Giant Sequoia trees are the fattest. They are so fat cars can drive through the trunk. There's no way to put them on a diet, though.

WAWONA

11

CALIFORNIA Says…

I have BIG Mountains called the Sierra Nevada.

The tallest mountain in the lower 48 states is my Mt. Whitney

at about 14,500 feet.

Alaska does have taller mountains.

And in my mountains are huge waterfalls.

The water plunges 2,425 feet from the top of Yosemite

Falls to the valley floor – the tallest in our country.

How tall are you *(name of child)*?

13

Cotton farming

CALIFORNIA Says...

Between my big mountains and huge Pacific Ocean are valleys.

The San Joaquin ("Wah-keen") River brings water to my Central Valley.

Farmers use the water to grow food and cotton.

Much of what you like to eat comes from my Central Valley.

14

CALIFORNIA Says…

The farmers grow… broccoli…carrots…lettuce…
onions…strawberries… tomatoes…nuts.
Name them and tell me which you like.

15

In my valleys farmers also raise turkeys, chickens and cows.

How much milk do you drink each day? *(child responds)*

Wow! That will make my cows happy to know they are helping you grow big and strong.

16

CALIFORNIA Says...

I also have famous valleys where the farmers grow grapes.

Many adults are happy that my Napa and Sonoma Valley have grapes.

Ask them what the grapes become after they are crushed.

17

I have some snow in many mountains all year round.

Do you have snow? Does it last all year?

CALIFORNIA Says…

This is Mt. Shasta. As you see, it is surrounded by green pine forests. Some of these trees are cut down to make lumber to build houses and other things.

Don't worry. When one tree is cut down a small tree called a sapling is planted immediately. My forests will always have lots of pine trees.

Douglas Fir Sapling

CALIFORNIA Says...

Just like you, my people need to drink water every day.

Since water only falls from my sky in winter and spring,

The rain and melted snow must be stored so my people can drink all year.

They learned to store the water by creating dams.

A dam creates a big lake by blocking the river.

Water flows through pipes from the lakes to your faucet.

When do you have rain *(name of child)* ?

Shasta Lake

19

CALIFORNIA Says...

Let me introduce you to some of my trees. We'll start where they have almost no rain at all...in the desert.

JOSHUA TREE Says...

I live in the desert and am called Joshua Tree.
I look big on top, but I don't fall over because my roots can go out over thirty feet underground.
My white flowers bloom in the Spring...but not every Spring.
It depends on how much rain I got during the year.
American Indians learned how to weave my leaves to make sandals or baskets.

Local Indians made a delicious meal out of my seeds and flower buds.

20

I am called Fan Palm…the only kind of Palm tree which grew
in California naturally. Other types of palms were brought in.
I live in the desert near Joshua. My green, fan-shaped leaves
are on top. My old leaves just hang down my trunk.
Many birds, insects and mice like to live amongst my old leaves.

21

MONTEREY CYPRESS Says...

I am Monterey Cypress. I live in a small area on California's
coast where the wind blows and shapes my branches.
I grow where the summers are cool but very moist.
I love being bathed by the fog from the sea.
It's believed I'm about two thousand years old!
How old are you?

You can eat my red berries.

They do look like tiny apples, don't they?

MANZANITA Says…

My name is Manzanita. It means "little apples" in Spanish.

You can find me near the ocean or in the mountains.

American Indians often used my leaves as a toothbrush.

If dry, my wood is great for fires and barbeques.

23

LIVE OAK Says...

I am called Live Oak because my leaves stay green all year. Other types of Oak lose their leaves in Fall.
Strong winds can't blow me over.
Squirrels, Quail, Wild Turkeys and
Whitetail Deer love my sweet acorns.

REDWOOD Says...

I'm Redwood. I only live near California's ocean where the air is moist and cool. The mist collects in my branches and falls to the ground as water. Then I can drink it.
I'm the tallest tree in the world and can live over two thousand years. Redwood forests are enjoyed by many birds, frogs, and animals. My wood is a beautiful red.

24

GIANT SEQUOIA Says...

I am the fattest tree in the world. I'm also very tall.

My name is Giant Sequoia.

I only grow in California's mountains.

My thick bark doesn't burn when there's a fire.

In fact fires are good for me. They destroy small trees and other growth clearing space around me and allowing me to live happily for a long time.

Some of us live over 3,000 years.

EAGLE *Says..*

I am Eagle, the king of birds. I soar high in the sky but I can see
even small things on the ground or fish in the water.

Here are few of California's other bird friends:

QUAIL *Says..*

Hi *(name of child)*! I'm Quail. I'm proud to be California's
state bird. Don't you like the tuft on top of my head?
What do you have on top of your head? I don't fly too much.
I like to stay on the ground, looking for yummy seeds.

26

CALIFORNIA CONDOR *Says..*

Hold on, Eagle, I've got the biggest wings of all birds... 9 feet.

(READER: take 10 steps toe-to-toe to show how far 9 feet is.)

I'm California Condor *(name)*. I'm very rare. I live on cliffs in only a few places in California. See me glide on the wind over the mountains and sea.

WILD TURKEY *Says..*

Recognize me? Yup, I'm Wild Turkey.

I'm only one of two types of birds that started in North America.

All the other birds came from some place else!

We live in flocks. Our flock sleeps in one or two trees.

Where do you sleep *(name)* ?

I can fly almost as fast as most cars go, but I prefer to walk or run.

I call to a lady turkey by gobbling. Can YOU gobble?

PELICAN *Says..*

Hi! I was Nigel in that "Nemo" movie.

Yes, I'm a Pelican. I have a pouch below my beak.

I use it to pick up fish so I can eat them or bring them back to my children.

I eat about four pounds a fish per day.

What kind of fish do you like?

HERON *Says...*

Heron here! I live near rivers, streams and the ocean...near my food.

My huge wings let me glide above the water as I hunt for fish.

I can stand still without moving for a long time. Can you *(name)* ?

SANDPIPER *Says..*

My name is Sandpiper.

My tiny legs and feet help me walk on top of the sand while hunting for insects.

28

GULL *Says..*

Hi, I'm Gull. Look at my feet.
They're sort of like swim fins you wear.
So I'm a good swimmer but would rather
wade near shore, looking for fish to eat.

29

BIG HORN SHEEP *Says...*

I'm Big Horn Sheep. I can climb up to places you, your mom and dad can't go! You might fall but I won't. I climb to avoid animals who might harm me. You wouldn't hurt me, would you *(name)*?

BEAR *Says...*

Hi you can call me Bear.

Like most bears I am big and VERY STRONG.

I can run, climb trees and swim. I sleep for many months.

How long do you sleep?

When I'm awake I must eat a lot of food...berries...fish.

What do you eat before sleeping?

RACCOON *Says...*

You can call me Raccoon.

Doesn't it look like I'm wearing a robber's mask?

My paws look something like your hands, don't they?

I learn mostly by feeling with my "hands".

I always wash my food before eating it. Do you?

BEAVER *Says...*

Beaver here! See my big flat tail. I slap it on water to warn other beavers of danger. I love to build with wood. My sharp teeth can cut down trees. I use them to build a dam or my home, called a "lodge". I love to build all the timc. That's why they call me a "Busy Beaver".

SKUNK *Says...*

I am Skunk. When I get scared I keep others away by raising my tail and spraying them with a bad smell. Eeeeuw Yuck! Be careful if you see me.

31

SEA LION *Says...*

I'm Sea Lion. I love to eat fish and play in the water.

My flippers are great for swimming but not good for walking on land.

I especially love to just lie in the sun with my friends.

WHALE *Says...*

We Whales are really big and swim in the ocean.

But I'm not a fish.

I must breathe air...like you...

and Otter and Sea Lion!

OTTER *Says...*

Hi *(name of child)*, Otters live in cold water so we have the thickest coat of fur of all the animals.

When I'm hungry, I lie on my back and crack a clam or oyster shell with a rock. Then I can eat.

How do you eat *(name)*? Lying on your back?

32

ELEPHANT SEAL *Says...*

You can call me Elephant Seal. Don't you like my nose? Looks sort of like an elephant, doesn't it?
I'm really big and can hold my breath for two hours when I dive down deep looking for food. After eating in the sea you can find me lying on the beach in the warm sun.

DOLPHIN *Says...*

Hi *(name)*, I'm Dolphin. I breathe air just like Whale.
I love to jump out of the waves. I'm really smart and can learn tricks that people teach me.
What tricks can you do?

SHARK *Says...*

I'm Shark. I can't ever sleep or I will sink to the bottom. I must swim all the time.
Do you sleep? Yes! Lucky you!
How long do you sleep?

33

CALIFORNIA *Says...*

Now, *(name of child)*, look how Mother Nature has made me so beautiful:

CALIFORNIA *Says...*

I have Lake Tahoe...the second deepest lake
in the whole United States.
Crater Lake in Oregon is deeper.
Sixty-three streams bring water into the Lake.
Only the Truckee River takes water out.

34

CALIFORNIA *Says...*

As the winter winds blow the clouds over my Sierra Nevada mountains - "Snowy Mountain Range" - deep snow collects on the mountain tops.

As the snow melts it creates fast-running rivers that tumble over huge cliffs on their way to my Pacific Ocean.

Some snow remains in the high-country even in late summer.

35

CALIFORNIA *Says...*

My Yosemite National Park has many spectacular waterfalls that plunge hundreds of feet. They include: Yosemite (2,425 feet), Bridalveil (620 feet) and Ribbon (1,612 feet)

They roar in May and June when the snow melts.

The falls trickle when it's dry in August and are reborn with autumn rainstorms.

El Capitan

Cathedral Spires

Half Dome

Bridalveil Falls

Yosemite Valley

This huge granite rock is called Half Dome.
It looks as though half of the dome was sliced away,
but it wasn't. Half Dome was "born" as you see it.
It's almost a mile above the Yosemite Valley floor.
It is so famous it is on the California quarter.

CALIFORNIA 1850

JOHN MUIR

YOSEMITE VALLEY

2005

E PLURIBUS UNUM

Half Dome

37

CALIFORNIA *Says...*

East of my mountains are dry deserts like Death Valley...
the lowest, driest and hottest place in the United States.
Only about two inches of rain falls each year. Sometimes none!
How much rain do you have where you live *(name of child)*?

Death Valley National Park

CALIFORNIA *Says...*

Notice the tracks behind that stone.
Death Valley has many moving/slidng rocks,
but no one has seen them move.
Some move hundreds of feet over time !

38

CALIFORNIA *Says...*

Death Valley is full of sand and amazing shapes.

Millions of years ago my land was deep under a salt sea.

The sea water evaporated, leaving large flat areas covered in salt.

When I have a tiny bit of rain, my desert blooms with color.

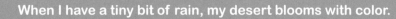

39

CALIFORNIA *Says...*

I have many natural harbors where fisherman safely store their boats when they're not out in my Ocean.

CALIFORNIA *Says...*

Last on our tour is my jagged coast line with trees clinging to rocks.

Occasionally sand beaches appear.

In the Big Sur area my coastal mountains disappear into the sea.

Man created a scenic highway with beautiful bridges to allow you to

sample my unique landscape.

CALIFORNIA *Says...*

Of all the places you've just seen,

which do you think is the most beautiful?

41

The first people on my land were small families of American Indians.

They grew vegetables and fished to feed their families.

Spain "owned" all my land. Its King ordered Spanish monks on a mission…

to convert my first people to Christianity. So Father Junipero Serra (U-ni-pear-oh)

and other friars started building missions near my Ocean.

In all, they created twenty-one missions.

The first people now provided food for themselves AND the friars at each mission.

42

CALIFORNIA *Says...*

The Esselen ("Eh-sa-len") and Ohlone ("oh-low-nee") Indians lived near the site of the future mission near Carmel.

They made the tools, roof tiles and adobe bricks needed to build the Mission.

Carmel Mission was the second one built by Father Serra.

The first Christian confirmation on my land took place here, as did the burial of Father Serra.

The Mission is an active parish church today.

Mission San Carlos Borromeo de Carmelo

Founded 1770

43

Mission Santa Barbara had three chapels built over time.

A huge earthquake in 1812 destroyed them. What you see now was opened in 1820.

Today she is known as the "Queen of the Missions" and is an active parish.

Built by the Chumash Indians, the Mission had an amazing water system.

It included two water reservoirs to store the water and aqueducts to transport it.

One of the reservoirs supplies the City of Santa Barbara with water to this day.

Mission Santa Barbara
Founded 1786

44

This mission served the Ohlone Tribe who farmed in the area.

The population in the area grew faster after this mission was constructed.

My land was originally called Alta California ("Upper California").

In 1821 Mexico took my land from Spain.

Now, more Spanish-speaking soldiers and citizens settled on my land.

My cities grew and grew – like you!

My biggest cities all have Spanish names.

Los Angeles means - *The Angels*

San Francisco means - *Saint Francis*

San Jose means - *Saint Joseph*

San Diego means - *Saint James*

Mission San Juan Bautista
Founded 1797

45

CALIFORNIA *Says...*

The United States bought my land from Mexico in 1848.

That year, in the foothills of my Sierra Nevada mountains, gold was discovered at Sutter's Mill and started the "California Gold Rush".

In 1849 prospectors began to flood in and my population exploded.

Sutter's Mill

46

Sluice Box

CALIFORNIA *Says...*

They used a pan to find gold in my streams. It's called "panning for gold."

You can still do it today.

Soon the people found a way to divert my river water into something called a "sluice."

It was much easier to find the gold that way.

47

In 1849 dreams of gold brought people from around the world.

150,000 arrived by ships at San Francisco. 150,000 came over land.

These new arrivals were called the "49ers".

In two short years San Francisco's population soared from 1,000 to 25,000.

FOR CALIFORNIA!
DIRECT
EXTRAORDINARY INDUCEMENTS!!
THIRTY-FIVE DAYS TO THE GOLD REGIONS!
The "California Steam Navigation Co."
Will dispatch their first vessel from New-York, the NEW and SPLENDID
STEAM SHIP!
NICARAGUA
DAVID JERROLD, Master, positively
On FRIDAY, MARCH 23d, 1849,
Via. the River St. Juan and Lake Nicaragua, across the Isthmus of Leon.
(Capt. BRONSON, of the U. S. Topographical Engineers)
200 JACK ASSES!
The Quickest, Safest and Cheapest!!
Price of Passage Through Ninety Dollars!

Many ships were abandoned in the harbor
as the captain and crew headed for gold country.

CALIFORNIA *Says...*

Now I had such a large population and vast resources, the United States invited me to become a state.

In 1850 I became the first state in the West.

Many people still came in ships. The first thing those travelers saw was the
entrance to San Francisco Bay. It was and is still called "The Golden Gate."

San Francisco Bay - 1849
"Golden Gate"

48

CALIFORNIA *Says...*

The building of a railroad stimulated my next growth spurt.

Many Chinese arrived to build the track for the first Transcontinental Railroad.

It was completed in 1869, making it easier for people to settle on my land and build new lives.

Today over 30 million people live here.

CALIFORNIA *Says...*

My land is actually on two parts of the earth's surface, called "plates".

One part, the Continental Plate, is part of our continent and is moving South.

The other is part, the Pacific Plate, is part of the ocean and is moving North.

The place where the plates meet is called a "fault line".

Here, enormous pressure builds between the plates.

The pressure is released as the plates suddenly shift, creating an earthquake.

Damage caused by earthquake

San Andreas Fault

50

In 1906 the Great San Francisco Earthquake destroyed buildings and started many fires. The fires did more damage than the earthquake because many buildings were made of wood and there was little water to put out the fires.

51

CALIFORNIA *Says...*

My people bounce back. San Francisco was rebuilt bigger and better.

Construction started on my Golden Gate Bridge in 1933.

After four years of battling winds, ocean currents and fog, it was finished.

**Golden Gate Bridge
under construction**

52

CALIFORNIA *Says...*

Today ships bringing goods to and from Asia and the rest of the world go under my Golden Gate Bridge.

It is one of the most beautiful structures built in the whole world.

What other buildings or structures do you think are more beautiful?

53

About the same time an important business was growing in Los Angeles...

Movies...and movie stars!

Hollywood is famous throughout the world for her movies and television shows.

Walk of Fame

54

Making movies in the 1920's

Shooting a TV show

CALIFORNIA Says...

Inside these big buildings there are sets, lights, costumes, actors and directors...
everything needed to make television shows and movies.

What are your favorite movies and why?

What are your favorite television shows and why?

CALIFORNIA *Says...*

While men and women make movies, buildings and bridges like the Golden Gate,

the most unique thing about me...California...is my natural beauty.

Sadly, many of my people don't take time to look at and enjoy what is right in front of them...

like the Channel Islands.

CALIFORNIA *Says...*

There are 145 types of plants and animals that can be found Nowhere

else in the whole wide world. That's pretty special, isn't it?

This area is a National Park, much of it under water.

Channel Islands National Park

56

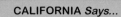

In the water is the largest animal on the earth...the Blue Whale.

They are over 100 feet long and can weigh over 150 tons (300,000 pounds).

Their tongues can weigh over 5,000 pounds!

How much do you weigh *(name)*?

Blue Whale and calf

57

My two volcanoes – Mt. Lassen and Mt. Shasta – are a reminder that below its crust the Earth still moves and is hot.

Right now my volcanoes are sleeping. Mt. Lassen was last "awake" about 100 years ago.

There are steam vents, volcanoes and earthquakes like mine throughout the world.

Mt. Lassen

Mt. Lassen erupts - May 15, 1915

Steam Vents

58

Mt. Shasta has been "sleeping" for over 200 years.

Each volcano will awaken again...when...no one knows!

In the meantime my volcanoes make me one of the most beautiful states in our country.

I've really enjoyed our time together *(name of child)*, but it's time for me to go. Before I do, see if you remember my tree, birds, ocean and animal friends.

What are they called?

HINT:

I'm on california's flag

HINT:

I eat on my back

HINT:

I have a "pouch" for fish

HINT:

I have flippers

HINT:

I am the tallest tree

HINT:

I am the state bird

HINT:

I breathe air

HINT:

my paws are like hands

60

I Am™ California

Adios... Bye...Bye.

61

Photographic & Other Credits

The Creators

Hugh Kennedy Tirrell

Photo: David Stephenson
avon sports.co.uk

Hugh grew up in New York State, was educated in Illinois, resided for 36 years is California, and currently lives in Arizona.

He has family in Maine, Massachusetts, Florida, Minnesota, and North Carolina, and has worked in or visited all but one of the other states. So, he has experienced many of the landmarks and cultures that make up America. He has been struck by the singular beauty of each state.

Through the years he conceived the idea of teaching children about the states—individually and collectively—by creating a series of books which enable children and their parents to learn together about the natural treasures and unique histories of our United States.

For 35 years Hugh has run an educational/motivational film production and distribution company.

He served as the Executive Producer, writer and director of over 60 films, many of them garnering national and international awards.

He continues to create Architect's Tours™ about famous golf courses.

Hugh shot most of the photographs used in each I AM AMERICA™ book.

Steven Gregory

Steven is the designer / digital artist behind the visual look and layout of each book in the I AM AMERICA™" series. He creates the landscapes and bring the plants and animals to life.

As owner and Creative director of Canal Street Studios in South San Francisco, CA, Steven designs and produces animation and special effects for television and film.

His clients include ad agencies, major league sports franchises and many fortune 500 companies.

Hugh and Steven have worked together on a number of DVD projects spanning several years.

Photography Credits

Many of the photos in this book were made my Hugh K. Tirrell

Photo of Lake Shasta on page 19 is courtesy of the Redding Convention & Visitors Bureau.

Photo of Blue Whale and Calf on page 57 is copyrighted by Philip Colla/Seapics.com and used with permission.

Photo of Miners on page 47 courtesy of Placer County Museums.